DAD'S JOKE ARSENAL

Over 900 Jokes Guaranteed to Make You Sigh

Copyright © 2025

Dad's Jokes

Over 900 Groaners That'll Make You Regret Turning the Page

All rights reserved. No part of this publication may be reproduced, distributed, or transmitted in any form or by any means, including photocopying, recording, or other electronic or mechanical methods, without the prior written permission of the publisher, except in the case of brief quotations used in reviews, blogs, or articles.

This is a work of humor. All jokes are fictional, pun-believable, and not meant to be taken seriously (except by dads, they take everything too seriously). Any resemblance to actual people, living or grilling, is purely coincidental.

ISBN: 978-1-956369-17-5

DEDICATION

For my kids,
who have endured these jokes their entire lives
and somehow still pretend to laugh.

And for every dad who thinks he's the funniest person in the room
You're not wrong… but you're definitely not right either.

Keep the puns alive.
The world needs your cringe.

NOTE FROM DAD

Hi there.
I'm Dad.

Now, I know what you're thinking:
"Do we really need another book of dad jokes?"

Yes. Yes, we do.

Because while the world may change…
While phones get smarter, music gets weirder,
and pants keep getting skinnier, there's one thing that never goes out of style: A painfully terrible dad joke.

These jokes?
They've been handcrafted, test-driven on eye-rolling teenagers,
and approved by at least one uncle at a barbecue.
They are clean, cheesy, and absolutely guaranteed
to make you groan loud enough for your neighbors to hear.
So grab your socks and sandals,
tighten your grip on that coffee mug that says "#1 Dad,"
and prepare yourself…

It's about to get punbelievably ridiculous.

You're welcome.
 Dad

Table of Content

The Dad Joke Commandments	1
Section 1: Dad at the Dinner Table	3
Section 2: Dad Logic 101	18
Section 3: Work, Tools & Other Excuses	33
Section 4: Animal Instincts	47
Section 5: Punbelievable	62
Section 6: DAD VS THE INTERNET	77
Dad's Joke Hall of Shame	92
Official Dad Joke License	98

THE DAD JOKE COMMANDMENTS

As passed down from the ancient scrolls hidden behind the lawnmower…

1. Thou shalt never miss an opportunity to pun.
Even if no one asks, especially when no one asks.

2. Thou shalt repeat the joke louder when no one laughs.
Because volume = comedy.

3. Thou shalt pause dramatically before delivering the punchline.
It's all in the timing.

4. Thou shalt always deliver jokes during serious moments.
Weddings. Job interviews. Dentist appointments. Strike when it's most awkward.

5. Thou shalt find great joy in groans, sighs, and facepalms.
That's the laugh behind the laugh.

THE DAD JOKE COMMANDMENTS

6. Thou shalt own at least one mug that says "#1 Dad."
It's a legal requirement for this kind of humor.

7. Thou shalt believe every joke is better the second... third... or tenth time.
Repetition makes perfection (or irritation).

8. Thou shalt consider yourself the funniest person in the room.
Even when you're alone.

9. Thou shalt sneak at least one pun into every conversation.
Because subtlety is for cowards.

10. Thou shalt pass on the sacred art of cringe to future generations.
One terrible joke at a time.

SECTION 1
Dad at the Dinner Table

Where the food's hot, and the jokes are... undercooked.

Dad at the Dinner Table

1. I made a pun about pizza…
But it was too cheesy.

---

2. Kid: "Dad, I'm hungry."
Dad: "Hi Hungry, I'm Dad."
(It's the law—I must say it.)

---

3. I only eat tacos on days that end in 'Y.'

---

4. "I burned the salad again…
I guess I still need to lettuce learn."

---

5. "I'm on a seafood diet.
I see food and I eat it."

---

6. "You can't trust a steak.
They're always a bit too rare."

---

7. "Fridge light turns off when you close the door?
Sounds like a job for a dad detective."

---

8. "Why did the grape stop in the middle of the road?
It ran out of juice."

---

9. "You left a spoon in the microwave again?
That's how time travel starts, kid."

---

10. "I tried to cook spaghetti in the washing machine.
Let's just say we're ordering pizza tonight."

Dad at the Dinner Table

11. "Milk expired? Nah.
It's just aged dairy."

---

12. "I named the fridge 'Titanic' because it's full of icebergs."

---

13. "Eggs are nature's little jokes.
Always cracking me up."

---

14. "I don't snack at night.
I conduct pantry investigations."

---

15. "Your mom asked me to stop making breakfast puns.
*I said I can't—I'm egg-cited to start the day."

---

16. "Dinner's ready when the smoke alarm goes off."

---

17. "Why did the toast break up with the butter?
It just couldn't spread the love anymore."

---

18. "I was going to make a joke about butter…
But I figured I'd spread it later."

---

19. "We're out of cereal?
This is a grain tragedy."

---

20. "I told the waiter I wanted my steak rare.
He brought it on a leash."

Dad at the Dinner Table

21. "I asked your mom what she wanted for dinner. She said 'something edible.' The pressure was immense."

22. "This soup tastes like it's keeping secrets."

23. "They said I couldn't make a joke about leftovers. But I reheated the idea."

24. "Why don't eggs tell each other secrets? They might crack under pressure."

25. "There's a slice of cake missing? Must be the work of the Midnight Snacker."

26. "I told the waiter I wanted a little seasoning. He brought me a tiny jazz band."

27. "I tried to make pancakes shaped like your mom's face. Now the smoke alarm calls me Picasso."

28. "When life gives you lemons, ask for salt and tequila."

29. I offered my sandwich a raise it said, "I already have bread."

30. Our spoons started arguing over who stirs up trouble more.

Dad at the Dinner Table

31. "I told your mom I'd make dinner.
She said cereal doesn't count."

---

32. "Who needs Michelin stars when you have Dad's Special?"

---

33. "I don't eat late at night.
I perform fridge raids."

---

34. "You wanted a light dinner,
so I served ice cubes and disappointment."

---

35. "I don't always burn dinner.
Just when I'm awake."

---

36. "I made a casserole.
Short for catastrophe roll."

---

37. "Why did the tomato turn red?
Because it saw the salad dressing!"

---

38. "Cooking tip: If you drop it on the floor, it's now stir-fry."

---

39. "I grilled the steak to perfection... if you like leather."

---

40. "Your cereal has no milk?
It's dry humor."

Dad at the Dinner Table

41. "Coffee isn't a beverage.
It's a survival ritual."

---

42. "What do you call a sad cup of coffee?
Depresso."

---

43. "Cooking is like jazz.
I never follow the sheet music."

---

44. "Leftovers are just food that's matured with experience."

---

45. "I once cooked dinner on the car engine.
Best drive-thru I ever had."

---

46. "I don't need a recipe.
I have overconfidence and hunger."

---

47. "Don't touch that plate!
It's dad-temperature: lava."

---

48. "I tried to make soufflé.
Now we have ceiling omelette."

---

49. "My secret ingredient is... panic."

---

50. "We're out of ketchup?
Cancel dinner. This is a crisis."

Dad at the Dinner Table

51. "Hot sauce isn't hot unless you scream mid-bite."

---

52. "I dropped the meatloaf.
Now it's streetloaf."

---

53. "Salads are just crunchy guilt."

---

54. "Ever tried air-frying toast in a hair dryer?
Don't."

---

55. "I call this dish: Suspicious Lasagna.

---

56. I made a salad pun once… but it just didn't lettuce be great.

---

57. I accidentally grilled my phone. Now it has Bluetooth.

---

58. The baker quit his job. He couldn't make enough dough.

---

59. I asked the waiter if the sushi was fresh. He said,
"It's still swimming in compliments."

---

60. My toast doesn't like mornings. It always crumbs under pressure.

Dad at the Dinner Table

61. I tried a seafood diet... I see food, and I eat it.

62. Our oven's on strike. It said it's too hot to handle.

63. The grapes started whining, I told them to stop wining.

64. I buttered you up... now will you pass the real butter?

65. I once dated a girl who worked at a bakery... she was a real flake.

66. The soup asked for attention. It needed to stew on something.

67. My fridge broke. I guess it just couldn't keep it cool.

68. I asked the apple if it wanted to go out. It said, "I'm feeling core-geous today."

69. The rice started gossiping, now we've got a real stir-fry going.

70. The steak told me to rarely underestimate it.

Dad at the Dinner Table

71. I brought a pie chart to dinner, it was well-rounded.

---

72. My diet starts tomorrow… just like it did yesterday.

---

73. If eggs had a podcast, it'd be called Crackin' Up.

---

74. My favorite subject in school? Lunch.

---

75. Don't trust tacos on Tuesdays. They always spill the beans.

---

76. That burger was so good, I'm now in a committed relish-tionship.

---

77. I made spaghetti. It was pasta-tively amazing.

---

78. The cereal had too many issues… it was a real flake.

---

79. I told the mashed potatoes they were smashing.

---

80. The ketchup bottle told me it was under pressure.

Dad at the Dinner Table

81. I tried to write a cookbook... but all the chapters were half-baked.

82. My kids asked if we had snacks. I handed them air-fried sarcasm.

83. If you microwave a joke, is it a hot take?

84. I used to be a spoon... but I couldn't handle the pressure.

85. I made coffee so strong it started lifting weights.

86. I opened a restaurant called "Guess What's for Dinner." We get a lot of confused customers.

87. Our dog ate the groceries again. He's paws-itively full.

88. I made a pun about oranges... but it never peeled right.

89. I took my sandwich to therapy. It had too many layers.

90. I tried making bread but it didn't rise to the occasion.

Dad at the Dinner Table

91. The ice cream asked me to chill.

92. I spilled milk and cried. I broke the cardinal rule.

93. The banana slipped up again.

94. I told the soup a joke. It was too salty to laugh.

95. My sandwich started a podcast. It's called "Let's Wrap It Up."

96. The microwave beeped in Morse code. I think it's sentient now.

97. I gave my burger a pep talk. It was feeling grilled.

98. My coffee walked out on me. Said I wasn't its type.

99. The donuts are hole-heartedly delicious.

100. The oven told me I kneaded a break.

Dad at the Dinner Table

101. Why did the salad go to therapy?
It had too many layers.

---

102. I burnt my Hawaiian pizza last night…
I should've used aloha temperature.

---

103. My eggs are always confident.
They never crack under pressure.

---

104. Why don't eggs tell jokes?
They'd crack each other up.

---

105. I opened a bakery that only sells bagels.
Business is holesome.

---

106. My coffee told me a joke this morning.
It was a real brewtal pun.

---

107. I made a pun about cereal once…
It was grrreatly underappreciated.

---

108. I told the waiter I wanted something light.
He brought me a candle.

---

109. My sandwich asked me for a raise.
I said, "You're already full of baloney."

---

110. The cheese and the bread got married.
It was a gouda match.

Dad at the Dinner Table

111. I made soup yesterday.
It was souper.

---

112. I invented a spoon that tells jokes.
It's a laughable utensil.

---

113. I tried eating the clock again.
It's still time-consuming.

---

114. Never trust tacos on Tuesday.
They always shell out lies.

---

115. I bought a cookbook called "Cooking for Dads."
It's just 100 ways to order takeout.

---

116. My rice made a joke yesterday.
It was a grain of comedy.

---

117. The grapes started fighting at dinner.
It turned into a raisined voice match.

---

118. I told the turkey it was overcooked.
It got roasted twice.

---

119. My fridge has commitment issues.
It always runs when I open up.

---

120. The banana slipped up on stage.
It didn't peel good.

Dad at the Dinner Table

121. The kitchen sink said, "I'm drained." I said, "Same, buddy."

122. I asked the blender how it was doing. It said, "I'm just going through a rough mix."

123. I caught the cheese talking behind my back… what a muenster.

124. My rice cooker gave me the cold shoulder. We're in a heated argument.

125. My fridge light flickered… I think it's trying to communicate.

126. I told my kids the broccoli was tiny trees. They deforested dinner.

127. The cookies staged a rebellion. I called it a smart cookie uprising.

128. I bought a cookbook titled "How to Burn Water"… finally, something I relate to.

129. The pancakes formed a band. Their hit single? Flippin' Awesome.

130. My dinner ran away. It said I was too clingy.

Dad at the Dinner Table

131. The lasagna told me, "Layer me gently."

---

132. The toaster's been quiet lately. Might be feeling crumby.

---

133. I served meatballs at a meeting, now it's a spaghetti conference.

---

134. My son said the rice was bland. I told it to spice up its life.

---

135. The dishwasher's on strike. It says it's not paid enough to soak drama.

---

136. Our carrots started meditating. They said they want to find their inner root.

---

137. I left soup on the stove and now it's hot gossip.

---

138. The milk jug gave me the coldest stare.

SECTION 2
Dad Logic 101

Why be right when you can be dad-right?

Dad Logic 101

1. "If your nose runs and your feet smell,
You're built upside down."

---

2. "I told your mom I'd fix the sink yesterday.
No need to remind me every six months."

---

3. "Why pay for therapy when I can just ignore my feelings like a man?"

---

4. "I don't make mistakes.
I create unexpected learning opportunities."

---

5. "If it ain't broke…
Give it to me. I'll break it trying to fix it."

---

6. "You don't need directions.
You need adventure."

---

7. "I'm not lost. I'm exploring the scenic route to the grocery store."

---

8. "Money can't buy happiness…
But it can buy duct tape. Same thing."

---

9. "If you fall, I'll always be there.
The Floor"

---

10. "I didn't forget your birthday.
I just wanted to make it more surprising."

Dad Logic 101

11. "Back in my day, we didn't have screens.
We stared at the wall and we liked it."

12. "Why take a nap when you can just fall asleep sitting up mid-sentence?"

13. "I don't need instructions.
I have instincts—and a toolbox full of wrong guesses."

14. "Do as I say, not as I confusingly do."

15. "If you're cold, put on a sweater.
Don't touch the thermostat. That's sacred."

16. "We don't call it laziness in this house.
We call it 'strategic resting.'"

17. "I'm not yelling, I'm just speaking with parental intensity."

18. "I didn't lose my hair.
It just migrated to my back."

19. "I don't snore.
I dream loudly."

20. "Sleep is for the weak.
That's why I take power naps instead."

Dad Logic 101

21. "I'm not ignoring you.
I'm giving your words time to age, like fine dad wine."

---

22. "Measure once. Cut five times. Still too short."

---

23. "I'm not cheap.
I'm fiscally dramatic."

---

24. "When I say 'five more minutes,'
You better start prepping for an hour."

---

25. "If you don't finish your food,
You're just giving future-you cold leftovers to regret."

---

26. If the light's not turning on, hit it once. If that fails, hit it twice.
Welcome to dad logic.

---

27. If I can fix it with duct tape, it's not broken, it's "creatively secure."

---

28. "Measure once, eyeball the rest." – Ancient Dad Proverb.

---

29. Why replace it when you can make it work... kinda... almost?

---

30. If I don't know what that button does, I press it anyway.
For science.

Dad Logic 101

31. The grill isn't hot until I burn off an eyebrow. Then it's ready.

32. If it's not making a noise yet, it's fine. Probably.

33. I taught your brother how to swim by throwing him in. You're next.

34. The thermostat is not a suggestion. It's a way of life.

35. If it squeaks, ignore it until it becomes part of the family soundscape.

36. Why ask for directions when I can get creatively lost?

37. I don't lose socks. They evolve into dryer gremlins.

38. Anything is a hammer if you hit it hard enough.

39. If I leave a project halfway done, it's because it's a "concept piece."

40. I told you not to touch it, now you've learned. That's called education.

Dad Logic 101

41. Instructions are just suggestions for the weak.

42. Why go to the doctor when I have Google and a stubborn immune system?

43. The best way to find something you've lost is to buy a new one.

44. If I say "Be there in five minutes," it means sometime today.

45. I don't need a manual. I have my instincts and poor judgment.

46. If it's not broken, I probably still took it apart to "see how it works."

47. I don't trust anything that doesn't rattle at least a little.

48. Tighten it until it cracks. Then back off a quarter turn. boom, fixed.

49. If I nod during your long explanation, I'm 50% listening, 50% thinking about snacks.

50. Want something done right? Ask me. Then I'll Google how to do it wrong.

Dad Logic 101

51. I told you I was resting my eyes, not napping. There's a difference.

52. I didn't forget, I was just letting you remember it on your own.

53. The garage is not messy. It's a "creative workspace."

54. If you can't find it, I'll come find it in 3 seconds using Dad Vision.

55. I wasn't lost. I was exploring alternate routes.

56. Why would I label wires when I can guess and hope for the best?

57. When I say "that's interesting," it means I don't agree and I'm planning my rebuttal.

58. I eat burnt toast because I don't waste food, I build character.

59. That switch? I don't know what it does, but I flipped it anyway. We'll find out soon.

60. If it survived a fall, it's durable. If it broke, it wasn't worth keeping.

Dad Logic 101

61. "Don't tell your mother" is not a request, it's survival.

62. Every dad has a drawer full of random things we'll need "one day." It's sacred.

63. The mower isn't loud, it's passionate.

64. Did I unplug it and plug it back in? Son, I invented that solution.

65. I once fixed a chair with gum and faith. It lasted two years.

66. I don't read instructions, I wrestle with failure until it makes sense.

67. If I grunt while standing up, I'm not in pain. I'm announcing my authority.

68. I told the remote it was grounded. It started working again. Fear works.

69. If I say "this'll only take five minutes," cancel your whole day.

70. Why hire a professional when I can do it wrong three times for free?

Dad Logic 101

71. Yes, I wear socks with sandals, it's called "advanced comfort."

72. Thermostat set at 72? That's criminal activity in this house.

73. I don't lose things. I strategically misplace them for future discovery.

74. If something smells funny, I'll sniff it twice, just to be sure.

75. "Because I said so" is backed by centuries of Dad science.

76. The lawn isn't mowed unless I sweat and feel slightly betrayed by the sun.

77. I wave at neighbors I don't like. That's how you stay mysterious.

78. My favorite tool is the hammer. If it doesn't fit, hammer it. If it breaks, hammer it again.

79. I take pride in driving with the gas light on. That's adrenaline parenting.

80. If I mutter under my breath during a project, that's part of the process.

81. I can fix it with duct tape, zip ties, or disappointment.

---

82. If I open the fridge and can't see it, it doesn't exist.

---

83. I won't ask for directions, that's an emotional trap.

---

84. My "back in my day" stories are 87% exaggerated and 100% law.

---

85. I don't do "small talk." I do "loud sighs and tool facts."

---

86. If I fix something, it stays fixed... until I touch it again.

---

87. I measure twice, cut once, then adjust five times.

---

88. Every dad has a special chair. Sit in it, and you'll awaken the ancient spirits.

---

89. I judge other dads based on how straight they edge their lawn.

---

90. I didn't lose hair, I gained aerodynamic wisdom.

91. That "junk drawer"? It's my hardware archive.

---

92. The grill isn't hot enough until it's legally dangerous.

---

93. My idea of a spa day is fixing something without being interrupted.

---

94. If I can't hear the TV, everyone has to be quiet. Even the microwave.

---

95. I trust my gut more than the manual. My gut has seen things.

---

96. If it's past 8PM, and I sit down. I'm not getting back up.

---

97. I label cables with tape, anger, and hope.

---

98. I consider yelling "I'm not mad, I'm just disappointed" a complete parenting strategy.

---

99. If someone touches the thermostat, I will rise from the dead.

---

100. I don't need a GPS. I need peace and quiet so I can get lost properly.

101. If a light switch doesn't work, I will flip it 20 more times just to be sure.

102. Why throw it out when I can keep it forever and never use it?

103. I'm not "tech-savvy," I'm "button-pressing until magic happens."

104. I didn't forget your birthday. I'm just letting the suspense build.

105. When I nod while you're talking, I'm either agreeing… or daydreaming about brisket.

106. Why fix the leaky faucet now? It's only been leaking for two years.

107. If I can open a jar with my bare hands, I'm stronger than 90% of the Avengers.

108. Every time I grill, I pretend I'm on a cooking show nobody asked for.

109. I use the phrase "back in my day" at least three times a week, and I regret none of them.

110. Silence in the car means I'm calculating gas mileage and judging traffic decisions.

111. That sigh I let out after sitting down? That's my soul rebooting.

112. If duct tape doesn't fix it, it wasn't meant to be fixed.

113. I make sure to let everyone know the Wi-Fi is acting up, even though I have no idea how it works.

114. The longer I stare at something broken, the closer I get to thinking I fixed it with my mind.

115. If you ask for help and I say "Give me a minute," that's dad code for "See you in an hour."

116. I don't actually know how to use all the tools in my toolbox. They're mostly emotional support.

117. If a dad grunts in the garage and no one hears it, did he really accomplish anything?

118. I believe in discipline, which is why I never let anyone touch my remote.

119. Asking me to find something in a cluttered drawer is a spiritual experience.

120. No one taught me how to dad-joke. It's an ancient instinct.

121. If something squeaks, I immediately go looking for WD-40 like a knight on a quest.

122. I believe every dad is born knowing how to use a plunger and yell at lawn equipment.

123. Don't question my methods. If it works, it's science.

124. If I had a dollar for every time I said "Because I said so," I could retire yesterday.

125. I treat "resting my eyes" like a sacred ritual. No, I'm not sleeping.

126. I can fix it, or at least make it someone else's problem.

127. I don't get lost. I just take scenic detours... sometimes for hours.

128. Every home project starts with three trips to the hardware store and a mild existential crisis.

129. If I can open the fridge and not find it, it doesn't exist. End of investigation.

130. When I say "I'll look into it," it goes into the same folder as "someday."

131. I'm not procrastinating. I'm strategically delaying for dramatic effect.

132. My phone's brightness is at max. My vision? Debatable.

133. I use full names when I'm serious, even with the dog.

134. Every "quick fix" turns into a weekend-long odyssey.

135. Nothing brings me joy like mowing straight lines into the lawn.

136. I read manuals like ancient scrolls. Mostly ignore them, but still read them.

137. If my kids are fighting, I just turn up the TV. Classic conflict resolution.

138. My default response to complaints is "Well, when I was your age..."

139. I call random things "doohickeys" when I forget the actual name.

140. I've spent more time adjusting the thermostat than I have on vacation.

SECTION 3
Work, Tools & Other Excuses

Work smart, not correctly.

Work, Tools & Other Excuses

1. "I told my boss I needed a raise.
He said, 'Why? Your jokes haven't improved.'"

---

2. "Why did the screwdriver go to therapy?
Too many twisted issues."

---

3. "If duct tape can't fix it,
You're not using enough duct tape."

---

4. "I don't have a 'man cave.'
I have a 'productivity-free zone.'"

---

5. "I once fixed a leak with chewing gum and blind hope."

---

6. "Measure once. Panic later."

---

7. "It's not broken.
It's just undergoing unplanned innovation."

---

8. "My resume is just a list of chores I didn't want to do."

---

9. "They said 'bring your best self to work.'
So I stayed home."

---

10. "I'm not procrastinating.
I'm letting the tools think about what they've done."

Work, Tools & Other Excuses

11. "Every time I touch a wrench,
A plumber gets their wings."

12. "My drill has two settings: Loud and Wrong."

13. "Work from home?
More like 'Hide from responsibilities.'"

14. "Why fix the faucet now...
When I can learn plumbing in 15–20 years?"

15. "Don't worry
I watched a YouTube video halfway through."

16. "Why do I own 3 hammers?
So I can lose two and still be disappointed."

17. "Office chair broke again?
Just means it respects my authority."

18. "I told HR my hands are full.
They didn't believe I meant with snacks."

19. "Yes, I'm 'between jobs.'
If you count being king of sarcasm as employment."

20. "It's not a mess.
It's a 'creative assembly zone.'"

Work, Tools & Other Excuses

21. "Why did the stapler get promoted?
Because it really held things together."

---

22. "I didn't lose the instruction manual.
I repurposed it into emotional support confetti."

---

23. "I treat every DIY project like a Marvel movie.
It starts exciting and ends with chaos."

---

24. "Honey, pass me the Allen key.
No idea who Allen is, but I need his help."

---

25. "Why mow the lawn now when nature can do it for free…
eventually?"

---

26. Wife: "Why is the shelf slanted?"
Me: "It's modern art."

---

27. Yes, I label my extension cords like my children. So I know which one not to trip over.

---

28. I only wear a tool belt to feel like Batman in cargo shorts.

---

29. I went to fix the sink. Now we need a new kitchen.

---

30. The lawn didn't need mowing. I just needed 45 minutes of peace and engine noise.

Work, Tools & Other Excuses

31. Boss: "Can you stay late?"
Me: "My dinner and my dignity say no."

---

32. Paint is dry when I say it's dry. Now sit back and admire the streaks.

---

33. If you haven't tripped over a hose, have you really lived?

---

34. I keep one tool rusty on purpose. It builds character.

---

35. The Wi-Fi went out at work, so we all just stared at each other like cave dads.

---

36. I said I'd fix it tomorrow. That was 47 yesterdays ago.

---

37. Drills don't ask questions. They just spin and scream like I do on Mondays.

---

38. My "office" is wherever no one can find me. Usually the bathroom.

---

39. Tool shopping counts as cardio. Have you seen me lifting a chainsaw?

---

40. My project isn't behind schedule, it's on dad time.

Work, Tools & Other Excuses

41. I didn't misplace the screwdriver. I relocated it creatively.

42. The shed isn't messy. It's a live exhibit of procrastination.

43. Yes, that's my third coffee. It's called project fuel.

44. If the job requires duct tape, I'm automatically overqualified.

45. I don't fix problems. I temporarily confuse them into submission.

46. Sawdust in my hair? That's my version of glitter.

47. I measure once, eyeball twice, and still blame the tape.

48. There are two settings on every power tool: "Off" and "Hold my root beer."

49. Wife: "Why are there seven hammers?"
Me: "They each have a specific mood."

50. I joined a Zoom call at work just to prove I was alive. Barely.

Work, Tools & Other Excuses

51. They said it's a team project. So I'm team "pretend I'm busy."

52. I once fixed a leak with bubble gum. Now I'm a legend in the plumbing group chat.

53. Don't touch my toolbox unless you want a five-part dad speech.

54. A wrench in the hand is worth two YouTube tutorials avoided.

55. I left the office early. Mentally. Around 10 a.m.

56. Ladders weren't made for comfort. They were made for dad-level danger.

57. I label cords like I label leftovers, with hope and confusion.

58. Glue guns aren't dangerous until dad gets "creative."

59. I don't overbuild. I prepare for apocalypse scenarios.

60. I didn't forget the deadline. I just emotionally rejected it.

Work, Tools & Other Excuses

61. I'm not avoiding the task. I'm visualizing the outcome... for hours.

62. If it doesn't fit, just hit it harder. That's engineering.

63. I went to the hardware store for one thing. Left with ten. That's the law.

64. The power drill isn't loud. It's just clearing its throat.

65. Why fix it today when I can avoid it with style?

66. I don't lose screws. I plant them around for future treasure hunts.

67. Boss: "Can you handle this?"
Me: "With duct tape and blind confidence? Absolutely."

68. My garage is where dreams and half-built shelves go to nap.

69. I didn't forget the nails. I just pre-decided on plan B.

70. Some dads wear ties to work. I wear sawdust and mild regret.

Work, Tools & Other Excuses

71. I don't call it a mess. I call it "creative chaos."

72. Work emails don't scare me. Replying to them does.

73. They asked for a minimalist approach. So I brought one hammer.

74. I said I was "on a job site." Technically, the lawn is a site.

75. If I ignore it long enough, maybe the leaking pipe will move out.

76. I've got a PhD in "pressing buttons until it works."

77. The only tool I truly trust is denial.

78. I didn't fall asleep on the job, I was resting my problem-solving face.

79. When in doubt, blame the blueprint.

80. Yes, I used the wrong wrench. But confidently.

Work, Tools & Other Excuses

81. I didn't forget the deadline. I just filed it under "eventually."

82. Every time I fix something, I break something else just to stay employed.

83. Measure twice, cut once, then stare at it confused for 20 minutes.

84. I don't make mistakes, I make "adjustable outcomes."

85. It's not a mess. It's a system that only I understand.

86. They said "wear protective gear." I thought they meant sarcasm.

87. A wrench in the hand is worth two in the junk drawer.

88. Work hard, nap harder. It's called balance.

89. I tighten screws until the wood apologizes.

90. Toolbox rule: If you can't find it, blame someone smaller.

Work, Tools & Other Excuses

91. Yes, I labeled the wires. No, I don't know what the labels mean.

92. My multitasking is mostly just switching between unfinished tasks.

93. I once built a birdhouse that scared birds. Still proud.

94. Work smarter, not harder. Or just complain until it fixes itself.

95. Some people have hobbies. I have half-painted garage walls.

96. Every tool has a story. Usually about how I used it wrong.

97. I could fix it... or I could dramatically sigh near it.

98. I didn't forget the job. I'm just building anticipation.

99. My drill bits are like socks, one always disappears mid-job.

100. I treat instructions like plot summaries: optional and mildly helpful.

Work, Tools & Other Excuses

101. I didn't lose the screwdriver. It's just hiding… in plain chaos.

---

102. If duct tape can't fix it, you're using too little.

---

103. I only cry in two places: funerals and when I drop a bolt in the engine.

---

104. I don't clock in. I just appear when coffee does.

---

105. I told my boss I'm working remotely. He didn't know I meant mentally.

---

106. Half my garage is tools. The other half is explaining why I needed them.

---

107. I wear my safety glasses to avoid seeing my mistakes clearly.

---

108. Ladders are just stairs for daredevils.

---

109. Work ethic? I prefer work aesthetics, looking busy without breaking a sweat.

---

110. They said "tighten until snug." I heard "twist until it screams."

Work, Tools & Other Excuses

111. I treat every screw like it owes me money.

112. If it's still wobbling, just call it "rustic."

113. Behind every great man is a project he swore he'd finish last summer.

114. I start every job with confidence and end it with a trip to the hardware store.

115. They asked if I had experience. I said, "I watched three YouTube videos."

116. I don't need a new drill. I just need to lose the old one again.

117. I once fixed a leaky faucet with duct tape, prayer, and overconfidence.

118. My boss asked if I could multitask. So now I pretend to work while actually working less.

119. I'm not procrastinating , I'm giving the project time to mature.

120. Measure twice, cut once, then blame the tape measure.

Work, Tools & Other Excuses

121. I didn't break it. It was just aggressively pre-disassembled.

122. The ladder isn't short, I'm just extra cautious when my life is 4 feet off the ground.

123. Every toolbox has that one mysterious key. I protect mine with my life.

124. Yes, I own 14 screwdrivers. No, I still can't find the right one.

125. My work-from-home setup includes a desk, a chair, and 6 snack breaks per hour.

126. I once fixed a squeaky door with cooking oil. It now smells like French fries.

127. If you can't fix it with duct tape, you haven't used enough duct tape.

128. I call it a "project" so I don't have to finish it for six months.

129. Wife: "Are you busy?" Me: "Let me grab a wrench and pretend to be."

130. Power tools make me feel like I have my life together.

SECTION 4
Animal Instincts

Because even the animal kingdom deserves dad jokes.

Animal Instincts

1. "What do you call a fish with no eyes? Fsh."

2. "I named our dog 'Five Miles' so I can tell people I walk Five Miles every day."

3. "Never trust a lion. They're always lion."

4. "I tried to train the cat to do chores. Now she just supervises me."

5. "You ever seen a lazy kangaroo? Yeah, they're pouch potatoes."

6. "I asked the owl how it feels. It said, 'Owl-right.'"

7. "What do you call a cow with no legs? Ground beef."

8. "What do you call a bear with no teeth? A gummy bear."

9. "I was chased by a group of flamingos once. It was a pink nightmare."

10. "Why did the squirrel bring a briefcase? He had nuts to attend to."

Animal Instincts

11. "Never wrestle a pig.
You both get dirty and the pig likes it."

12. "What did the dog say to the tree?
Bark."

13. "The chicken crossed the road to tell a dad joke.
Unfortunately, nobody egg-spected it."

14. "Why don't crabs give to charity?
Because they're shellfish."

15. "Our cat thinks she's royalty.
And honestly… we serve her like she is."

16. "I didn't adopt a dog.
I recruited a furry alarm system."

17. "The zoo called.
They want their jokes back."

18. "What do you call an alligator in a vest?
An investigator."

19. "There's a bird outside that mocks me.
Literally. It's a mockingbird."

20. "Our parrot left me for someone with better punchlines."

Animal Instincts

21. "What's a snake's favorite subject in school? Hissss-tory."

22. "I let the dog name the Wi-Fi. It's now 'Bark-Fi 2.0.'"

23. "I wanted to adopt a sloth. But the paperwork took three years."

24. "Don't play poker with a cheetah. They always spot your bluff."

25. "Why did the duck sit on the charger? It wanted to power up its quack."

26. I hired a dog to mow the lawn. All he did was bury the mower.

27. My cat just bought crypto. Now she's a meow-llionaire.

28. Why don't ducks tell jokes while flying? Because they might quack up midair.

29. The lion applied for a desk job. His resume just said "King."

30. My fish started a podcast. It's called Gill Talks.

Animal Instincts

31. I saw a snake doing yoga.
He was working on his hiss-teric flow.

32. Why was the pig always broke?
Because he kept going hog-wild on spending.

33. My lizard started doing TikTok dances.
He's now a rep-tile influencer.

34. The crow brought me a gift.
It was shiny, pointless, and confusing, just like my last relationship.

35. What did the bee say to the flower?
"I like your pollenality."

36. Why did the crab get promoted?
He had claws for celebration.

37. My parrot insulted me in Spanish.
I don't even know how he learned that.

38. What do you call a cow that plays guitar?
A moo-sician.

39. I tried to talk politics with my dog.
He just barked "No comment."

40. Why did the horse get fired from the office?
Because he kept saying "neigh" to every task.

Animal Instincts

41. Why did the owl fail his driving test?
He couldn't stop hooting at pedestrians.

---

42. My goat just got into law school.
He's going to be a baaa-rrister.

---

43. What do you call an ant who fights crime?
A vigil-ant-e.

---

44. I caught my hamster ordering stuff online.
Turns out he's got Amazon Prime-ates.

---

45. Why did the dolphin get kicked out of school?
Too many whale tales.

---

46. My pet chicken started a side hustle.
He's now selling eggs-traordinary NFTs.

---

47. What do you call a group of musical whales?
An orca-stra.

---

48. I asked the cat to do chores.
She stared, blinked once, and walked off like a queen.

---

49. Why did the kangaroo break up with the rabbit?
Too much bouncing around.

---

50. I saw a squirrel doing CrossFit.
Dude was ripped, probably benching acorns.

Animal Instincts

51. Why did the bear refuse dessert?
He was already stuffed.

---

52. I tried to train my dog to use the toilet.
Now he just sits on it and judges me.

---

53. The owl's dating advice?
"Don't give a hoot what they think."

---

54. Why did the zebra bring a ruler to the bar?
To measure his stripes of courage.

---

55. My fish ghosted me.
Turns out he was just being koi.

---

56. Why do pandas never argue?
Because they eat, sleep, and let bamboo things go.

---

57. I walked in on the dog watching Animal Planet.
He barked, "Don't change it, this episode's pawsome!"

---

58. Why don't pigs do karaoke?
They hate hogging the mic.

---

59. My horse just joined LinkedIn.
His profile says: "Driven. Fast. Grass connoisseur."

---

60. Why did the lobster bring a briefcase to dinner?
Because he meant claw-business.

Animal Instincts

61. Why don't snakes ever get lost?
They always follow their hiss-tincts.

62. I told my cat a joke.
She gave me a slow blink and walked off. Tough crowd.

63. Why did the sloth break up over text?
He said it was the fastest way.

64. My parrot started a podcast.
It's mostly just repeats though.

65. Why did the chicken cross the playground?
To get to the other slide.

66. I saw a frog at the ATM.
He said he was checking his ribbit balance.

67. Why was the giraffe late?
Because he was stuck in a tall tale.

68. What do you call a dog who designs websites?
A weboodle developer.

69. The cow started a meditation class.
It's called Moo-ndfulness.

70. Why don't pandas like fast food?
Because they can't catch it.

Animal Instincts

71. My turtle finally finished his book.
Took him six years, but hey, slow and storyful.

---

72. Why did the duck become a detective?
He always quacked the case.

---

73. I told my lizard to get a job.
He said, "I'm already in scales."

---

74. Why don't seagulls fly over the bay?
Because then they'd be bagels.

---

75. What do you call an alligator in a vest?
An investi-gator.

---

76. My bee joined a band.
He's the buzz guitarist.

---

77. Why did the cat enroll in yoga?
To work on her meow-stretching.

---

78. I asked my dog what's two minus two.
He said nothing. Exactly.

---

79. Why did the horse write a memoir?
Because he had a stable story to tell.

---

80. The bear got a new phone.
He said, "This thing has paws recognition!"

Animal Instincts

81. Why don't antelopes use social media?
Because they don't want to get hornswoggled.

---

82. My fish started a business.
He's now the CEO of Swimvestments.

---

83. Why did the owl break up with his girlfriend?
He said, "Owl be seeing someone else."

---

84. I opened a zoo.
It only has one animal, a dog.
It's a Shih Tzu-n.

---

85. Why did the crab never share?
Because he was a little shellfish.

---

86. The kangaroo failed his driving test.
He kept hopping lanes.

---

87. My goat joined a rock band.
He's the lead baa-ssist.

---

88. What do you get when you cross a cow and a trampoline?
A milkshake.

---

89. Why did the horse bring a ladder to the bar?
Because he heard the drinks were on the house.

---

90. The bat got kicked out of choir.
He was always off-key at night.

Animal Instincts

91. Why don't cheetahs play hide and seek?
Because they're always spotted.

92. I asked the dolphin if he wanted to hang out.
He said he was feeling a little salty.

93. The pig got promoted.
Now he's bringing home the bacon and the spreadsheets.

94. Why did the turkey start a fight?
Because someone said he was just stuffing.

95. My snake's jokes are never funny.
They always boa-ring.

96. The hamster opened a bakery.
Specializes in tiny rolls.

97. Why don't elephants use laptops?
They're afraid of the mouse.

98. What did the lion say before dinner?
"Let's make this roar-mantic."

99. I asked the octopus for directions.
It pointed in eight directions.

100. Why did the squirrel apply for a loan?
To invest in nutflix.

Animal Instincts

101. Why did the duck sit in the shade?
Because he didn't want to be a hot quack.

---

102. I tried to teach my cat to fetch.
Now he just fetches judgment.

---

103. What do you call a bear with no teeth?
A gummy bear.

---

104. Why was the giraffe late to work?
He got stuck in a high-level meeting.

---

105. The rabbit opened a spa.
Specialized in hare care.

---

106. Why did the donkey become a philosopher?
Because he always questioned bray-lity.

---

107. I adopted a parrot that only whispers.
Turns out it's a secretary bird.

---

108. Why did the lizard open a fast-food joint?
To serve rep-tizers.

---

109. What did the cow say during a breakup?
"This is udderly disappointing."

---

110. I saw a buffalo at the gym.
Dude was working on his bison-triceps.

Animal Instincts

111. The frog became a motivational speaker.
His topic? Leap into success.

112. Why did the spider get into tech?
Great at web design.

113. I trained my pigeon to deliver jokes.
It's a coo-median.

114. Why don't koalas start drama?
They prefer to leaf it alone.

115. My cat ran for office.
Her campaign slogan was "Paws for Change."

116. The peacock refused to share the mirror.
Said he needed time for self-reflection.

117. What's a snake's favorite dance move?
The hiss-ter slide.

118. The beaver started a construction company.
Business is dam good.

119. Why do flamingos always stand on one leg?
Because if they lifted both, they'd fall over.

120. I asked the owl for advice.
He just said, "Who?"

Animal Instincts

121. Why did the fox start a podcast?
Because he had tales to tell.

122. The turtle's comedy career is slow...
But shelly worth it.

123. Why don't moose use elevators?
They prefer to take it by the antlers.

124. The monkey started a YouTube channel.
It went bananas.

125. Why was the whale always invited to parties?
Because he brings the splash.

126. I asked the zebra for fashion tips.
He said, "Stay in line."

127. What do you call a crocodile in a vest?
An investi-gator.

128. Why did the porcupine get a restraining order?
Too many sharp remarks.

129. The lion became a therapist.
He listens with purr-pose.

130. Why don't penguins ever lie?
They're too cool for that.

Animal Instincts

131. The raccoon wrote a memoir.
Titled: "Trash But Classy."

132. Why did the bear buy a fancy car?
Because he wanted to go fur-st class.

133. The chameleon failed the exam.
He froze under pressure.

134. Why was the dog a terrible dancer?
He had two left paws.

135. The goldfish started journaling.
He's trying to find himself.

136. Why did the rooster join a rock band?
Because he was born to cock-a-doodle do it.

137. The cat broke up with me.
She said I lacked meow-tivation.

138. Why don't leopards play hide and seek?
Because they're always spotted.

139. The hippo became a food critic.
He only eats meals with real depth.

140. I told my dog a joke about squirrels.
He said, "That's nuts."

SECTION 5
Punbelievable

Wordplay so bad… it's punbelievable.

Punbelievable

1. "I was going to tell a time-travel joke...
But you didn't like it."

---

2. "I'm friends with all electricians.
We have good current connections."

---

3. "I used to be a baker,
But I couldn't make enough dough."

---

4. "I'm reading a book on anti-gravity.
It's impossible to put down."

---

5. "I used to be a banker...
Then I lost interest."

---

6. "I'm not lazy.
I'm on energy-saving mode."

---

7. "I once worked at a calendar factory...
But I got fired for taking a few days off."

---

8. "My math teacher called me average.
How mean!"

---

9. "I got a job as a human statue.
Needless to say, I'm still."

---

10. "What's orange and sounds like a parrot?
A carrot."

Punbelievable

11. "I asked the librarian if the library had books on paranoia. She whispered, 'They're right behind you.'"

12. "I told my suitcases there will be no vacation this year. Now I'm dealing with emotional baggage."

13. "Did you hear about the guy whose whole left side was cut off?
He's all right now."

14. "I failed math so many times I can't even count."

15. "Becoming a vegetarian was a big missed steak."

16. "Claustrophobic people are more productive thinking outside the box."

17. "Why don't skeletons fight each other?
They don't have the guts."

18. "I got hit in the head with a can of soda.
Luckily, it was a soft drink."

19. "I have a fear of speed bumps...
But I'm slowly getting over it."

20. "My ceiling isn't just a ceiling.
It's up there, doing its best."

Punbelievable

21. "I went to a seafood disco last night...
And pulled a mussel."

22. "I built a model of Mount Everest...
But it's all downhill from here."

23. "Did you hear about the guy who invented Lifesavers?
He made a mint."

24. "The shovel was a groundbreaking invention."

25. "I used to be a train driver...
But I got derailed."

26. I lost my job at the shoe factory. I just couldn't heel.

27. My math teacher called me average. How mean!

28. I'd tell a chemistry joke but I know I wouldn't get a reaction.

29. I started a company selling Velcro. It's a total rip-off.

30. I was struggling to figure out how lightning works, then it struck me.

Punbelievable

31. I wrote a play about puns. It's a pun-tingent performance.

32. I built a pun empire, but it collapsed due to wordplay inflation.

33. I'm terrified of elevators, so I take steps to avoid them.

34. I don't get people who hate puns. It's the lowest form of wit, and I dig it.

35. My dad joke career? It's punstoppable.

36. I bought a thesaurus, but all the pages were blank. I have no words.

37. I spilled herbicide on my poetry book. Now I've got dead prose.

38. I told my barber I was punstoppable. He gave me a cutting look.

39. I told my printer a joke, it jammed.

40. My jokes are all pun-derful. You're welcome.

Punbelievable

41. I quit my job at the helium factory. I refused to be spoken to in that tone.

42. I once got into a fight with a broken elevator. It was wrong on so many levels.

43. I bought a pair of camouflage pants. I can't find them now.

44. I asked the librarian if they had books on paranoia. She whispered, "They're right behind you..."

45. I'm reading a horror novel in Braille. Something bad is going to happen...I can feel it.

46. I got a job at a bakery because I kneaded dough.

47. I was struggling to figure out how lightning works... then it struck me.

48. I don't trust stairs. They're always up to something.

49. I used to play piano by ear, but now I use my hands.

50. The shovel was a ground-breaking invention.

Punbelievable

51. My friend got hit with a can of soda. Luckily, it was a soft drink.

52. I started a band called 999MB. We haven't gotten a gig yet.

53. I accidentally swallowed some food coloring. The doctor says I'm okay but I feel like I've dyed a little inside.

54. I told my wife she should embrace her mistakes… She gave me a hug.

55. I used to work for a blanket company, but it folded.

56. I once made a pun about vegetables. It was corny.

57. I got a new job at the orange juice factory, but I got canned… couldn't concentrate.

58. I had a joke about construction, but I'm still working on it.

59. I bought a ceiling fan. Complete waste of money. He just stands there and claps.

60. I opened a restaurant called "Karma." There's no menu, you get what you deserve.

Punbelievable

61. I tried to catch some fog yesterday. Mist.

62. I got a job as a human statue. I'm just going through a still phase.

63. I used to be addicted to soap… but now I'm clean.

64. I'm reading a book on anti-gravity. It's impossible to put down.

65. I don't trust atoms. They make up everything.

66. I opened a bakery for dogs. It's called "Pupcakes."

67. I was going to tell you a time-travel joke… but you didn't like it.

68. I bought a thesaurus, but when I got home, all the pages were blank… I had no words.

69. I told a joke about an elevator. It had its ups and downs.

70. I became a baker because I couldn't make enough dough as a musician.

Punbelievable

71. I named my new dog "Five Miles" so I can say I walk Five Miles every day.

72. My new diet plan? Don't eat anything that requires more than two syllables to pronounce.

73. I tried learning sign language. It's not my strong suit... I couldn't pick up the gestures.

74. I wanted to be a mirror installer... it's a job I could really see myself in.

75. I wrote a song about a tortilla. Well, it's more of a wrap.

76. I used to play piano by ear... but now I use my hands.

77. My friend's bakery burned down. Now his business is toast.

78. The shovel was a ground-breaking invention.

79. I don't really understand electricity... but I'm shocked by how powerful it is.

80. I bought a belt made of watches. It was a waist of time.

Punbelievable

81. I accidentally swallowed a dictionary. Now I'm at a loss for words.

---

82. The guy who invented autocorrect should burn in hello.

---

83. I used to be a banker, but I lost interest.

---

84. I once had a job at a calendar factory... but I got fired for taking days off.

---

85. I told my wife she was drawing her eyebrows too high. She looked surprised.

---

86. I changed my iPod's name to Titanic. It's syncing now.

---

87. I told a joke about a roof once... it went over everyone's head.

---

88. I got hit in the head with a can of soda. Luckily, it was a soft drink.

---

89. I know a guy who's addicted to brake fluid... but he says he can stop anytime.

---

90. I used to hate facial hair... but then it grew on me.

Punbelievable

91. I once dated a girl who was a tennis player, but love meant nothing to her.

92. I used to be indecisive… now I'm not sure.

93. I was going to tell a time-travel joke, but you guys didn't like it.

94. I'd tell you a construction joke… but I'm still working on it.

95. My math teacher called me average. How mean!

96. I once got locked in a bakery overnight. I felt crumby in the morning.

97. I opened a bakery that only sells bagels and puns. It's called "Hole-y Jokes."

98. I wrote a book on reverse psychology. Don't buy it.

99. I used to be afraid of hurdles, but I got over it.

100. I've started telling people about the benefits of dried grapes. It's all about raisin awareness.

Punbelievable

101. The guy who invented knock-knock jokes deserves a no-bell prize.

---

102. My new thesaurus is terrible. Not only is it terrible, it's terrible.

---

103. I don't trust stairs... they're always up to something.

---

104. I made a pun about the wind... but it blows.

---

105. I used to be addicted to soap... but I'm clean now.

---

106. I was struggling to figure out how lightning works... then it struck me.

---

107. I bought a ceiling fan the other day. Complete waste of money. All it does is stand there and clap.

---

108. I'm writing a book on anti-gravity. It's impossible to put down.

---

109. I started a business selling puns about clocks. It's about time.

---

110. I told my wife she was drawing her eyebrows too high. She looked surprised.

Punbelievable

111. I asked the librarian if the library had books on paranoia. She whispered, "They're right behind you."

112. I once swallowed a dictionary. It gave me thesaurus throat.

113. I told my plants a joke about photosynthesis. They were rooted to the spot.

114. I once tried to catch some fog… I mist.

115. I named my dog "Five Miles" so I can say I walk Five Miles every day.

116. I used to be a banker, but I lost interest.

117. I told my computer I needed a break. Now it won't stop sending me beach ads.

118. I tried to write a pun about vegetables, but it was too corny.

119. My dad told me I'd never make a pun about carpentry… but I nailed it.

120. I got hit in the head with a can of soda. Good thing it was a soft drink.

Punbelievable

121. I used to play piano by ear, but now I use my hands.

122. I made a pun about the wind, but it blew right over everyone's head.

123. I'd make a chemistry pun, but I know I wouldn't get a reaction.

124. I once dated a girl who was a tennis player… love meant nothing to her.

125. I couldn't figure out why the baseball kept getting bigger… then it hit me.

126. I asked the waiter if the steak was rare… he said, "Nah, we have it all the time."

127. I got a job at a bakery because I kneaded dough.

128. I bought a fake noodle. It was an impasta.

129. I've got a great joke about construction, but I'm still working on it.

130. I opened a bakery that only sells bagels shaped like infinity symbols. It's called "Forever Dough."

Punbelievable

131. I gave all my dead batteries away… free of charge.

132. I once told a joke about elevators. It had its ups and downs.

133. I'm no good at math, but I know one thing: 5/4 of people struggle with fractions.

134. I used to be addicted to the hokey pokey, but I turned myself around.

135. I made a belt out of watches. It was a complete waist of time.

136. I asked my friend if he wanted a frozen banana. He said no… but he wanted a regular one later, so I froze one just in case.

137. I told my shoes they were doing a great job. They're so sole-ful.

138. I invented a new word! Plagiarism.

139. I asked the gym instructor if he could teach me to do the splits. He said, "How flexible are you?" I said, "I can't make it on Tuesdays."

140. I didn't want to believe my dad was stealing from his job as a traffic cop… but when I got home, all the signs were there.

SECTION 6
DAD VS THE INTERNET

When Dad Logs On... and the world Logs Off.

Dad vs the Internet

1. I asked Google how to fix my lawnmower.
Now I'm signed up for a programming course.

---

2. I tried to connect to the family Wi-Fi.
It said: "Connection rejected, Dad joke detected."

---

3. Your mom said she wanted a smart TV.
So I sat in front of it with glasses and gave a TED Talk.

---

4. They said I need to update my browser.
So I shaved my mustache and got a new pair of shades.

---

5. I accidentally sent your mom a poop emoji.
Meant to send a heart.
Close enough, right?

---

6. My phone died.
I gave it mouth-to-USB.
Didn't work.

---

7. I tried Snapchat once.
Now my face is a hotdog in the cloud somewhere.

---

8. Told your uncle I'm "offline."
He said, "Oh, like your fashion sense?"

---

9. They asked me for my email.
I wrote: "Yes please."

---

10. Just Googled "how to Google things."
Step one: don't tell anyone you just did that.

Dad vs the Internet

11. They told me to use cloud storage.
So I uploaded my photos… into the sky.
Literally.

---

12. The Wi-Fi went out.
We had to talk to each other.
It was terrifying.

---

13. Your grandma just DM'd me.
Should I be worried?

---

14. Tried to use Face ID while eating donuts.
Phone said: "Try again when you've cleaned your face, sir."

---

15. I told the TV to turn on.
It laughed.
Now I sleep with one eye open.

---

16. Autocorrect changed "Hi honey" to "Hit homey."
Now your mom's not speaking to me.

---

17. Downloaded a fitness app.
Uninstalled it immediately when it asked me to move.

---

18. The only cookies I accept…
Are chocolate chip.

---

19. They said I needed a firewall.
So I built one.
With bricks. In the garage.

---

20. Your mom asked if I'd ever go viral.
Told her I already did in 1982. Chickenpox.

Dad vs the Internet

21. My laptop froze,
so I yelled "Let it go!"
Still frozen.

---

22. Got an email saying I won $1 million.
All I had to do was send my bank details.
Guess who's rich now?
(Not me.)

---

23. Tried TikTok.
Now I have a headache, a dance injury, and no followers.

---

24. Your mom asked what VPN is.
I said "Very Powerful Netflix."

---

25. Tried voice typing.
Now my grocery list says "Goat cheese astronaut pants."

---

26. Reset my password.
New one: "YouKidsGetOffMyLawn123!"

---

27. Asked Siri to play classic rock.
She played Justin Bieber. I filed a complaint.

---

28. Your mom said we need antivirus.
I gave her orange juice and a nap.

---

29. I opened a Twitter account.
Still haven't figured out what a thread is.
I just want to talk about socks.

---

30. Updated my bio to say "Legend."
No likes. Just judgment.

Dad vs the Internet

31. Tried to update my status.
Updated my marital status by mistake.
Your mom isn't amused.

---

32. Instagram suggested "hot dads near you."
It was just me in a mirror.

---

33. Said I was "in the cloud."
Wife handed me an umbrella.

---

34. Got a smartwatch.
It buzzed when I stood up.
Felt judged.

---

35. Asked Alexa to tell me a joke.
She said, "Your haircut."

---

36. Used a filter on my face.
App crashed.

---

37. I posted a selfie.
Your grandma commented, "Who is this?"

---

38. Zoom meeting started.
Camera showed only my forehead.
Professionalism: achieved.

---

39. Tried to react with a fire emoji.
Sent a fire truck instead.

---

40. Sent your mom a GIF.
Now she thinks we're breaking up.

Dad vs the Internet

41. My Wi-Fi password is "StopAskingMeForTheWiFi."

---

42. I clicked "I Agree" without reading.
Now I own a goat in Bolivia.

---

43. Tried to clear my browser history.
Cleared my whole childhood.

---

44. Tried Bluetooth headphones.
Now I talk louder because I can't hear myself.

---

45. They asked if I stream.
I said, "Only when it rains."

---

46. The Internet said I was wrong.
So I unplugged it.

---

47. Typed "Dad" in Google.
It asked, "Did you mean Legend?"

---

48. Sent your mom a romantic text.
Accidentally sent it to my boss.
Still got a heart emoji though.

---

49. Logged in as Guest.
Felt like royalty.

---

50. I backed up my phone.
Now it won't stop beeping at me.

Dad vs the Internet

51. I joined Reddit.
Now I have opinions I didn't know I had.

52. I clicked "Remember Me."
My computer forgot me the next day.

53. I asked ChatGPT for advice.
It told me to stop telling dad jokes.
I reported it.

54. Used Incognito Mode.
Still got caught watching cat videos.

55. The printer is out of ink.
Again.
I think it's messing with me.

56. Signed up for a password manager.
Forgot the password to it.

57. Accidentally posted on your mom's Facebook.
Now all her church friends think I'm into skateboarding.

58. Autoplay on YouTube took me from cooking rice…
to ancient Viking battles.

59. I clicked a link.
Now my screen has sparkles and salsa music.

60. Asked the AI fridge what's for dinner.
It said "Ice."

Dad vs the Internet

61. Posted one meme.
Now I'm the family meme dealer.

---

62. I downloaded an app to help me sleep.
It screamed at me to go to bed.

---

63. The toaster is now smart.
It rejected my bread.

---

64. I left a Zoom call by saying,
"I'm buffering."
It worked.

---

65. Googled "How to act cool."
Ended up buying a leather jacket.

---

66. I used a dad filter.
It just zoomed in on my socks.

---

67. I joined a group chat.
Now I get 200 messages about rice every hour.

---

68. I tried online banking.
Now I'm broke, but digitally.

---

69. I asked Siri where I left my keys.
She said, "I don't know, ask your wife."

---

70. I clicked "Accept Cookies."
Still waiting.

Dad vs the Internet

71. I created a TikTok account.
Now it wants me to dance.
That's a crime.

---

72. My phone keeps updating.
It's smarter than me now.

---

73. Asked Alexa for a bedtime story.
She played heavy metal.

---

74. I tried VR.
I punched the dog.

---

75. Googled "How to talk to teens."
It said, "Don't."

---

76. I posted a story on Instagram.
Now I'm a storyteller.

---

77. My smart fridge judged me for taking ice cream at 2 AM.

---

78. Bought a ring light.
Now I just look like a shiny potato.

---

79. Autocorrect changed "I'm proud of you"
to "I'm prawn of you."

---

80. I set a screen time limit.
Then ignored it.

Dad vs the Internet

81. My phone has Face ID.
Refuses to open before coffee.

---

82. Tried to mute a group chat.
Muted myself instead.

---

83. Got a smartwatch for fitness.
Now it insults me hourly.

---

84. Typed "LOL" by accident.
Now I'm in a gaming clan.

---

85. The internet went out.
I rediscovered... sunlight.

---

86. Made a meme about my back pain.
Went viral.
Now I have merch.

---

87. I said "OK Boomer" to Alexa.
She shut down.

---

88. Tried to Google "how to delete cookies."
Now I'm just hungry.

---

89. I joined Discord.
Still no idea what I agreed to.

---

90. Voice search heard "nachos" instead of "notches."
Best mistake ever.

Dad vs the Internet

91. Tried sending a Bitmoji.
Sent a potato in space instead.

---

92. Signed up for TikTok to stay relevant.
Now I need a chiropractor.

---

93. I tried tagging your mom.
Accidentally tagged my ex.

---

94. I put my phone on dark mode.
Now it's moody.

---

95. Your sister asked for a new mouse.
I gave her a pet store receipt.

---

96. Signed up for a cooking channel.
Now the kitchen's on fire.

---

97. My podcast has one listener.
It's me.
On repeat.

---

98. Subscribed to 20 newsletters.
Now my inbox has trust issues.

---

99. Posted a dad joke.
Got blocked by my son.

---

100. Asked the AI assistant for life advice.
It suggested yoga and less dad jokes.

Dad vs the Internet

101. Tried to join TikTok.
Accidentally joined a knitting forum.
Now I make scarves.

---

102. Your mom said I spend too much time on Facebook.
So I blocked her.

---

103. Updated my phone.
Now I can't find anything… Including my dignity.

---

104. The kids say I don't understand memes.
That's their problem, not mine.
Insert frog sipping tea.

---

105. Signed an email:
"Best regards, Dad."
To Amazon customer support.

---

106. Tried to scan a QR code at the restaurant.
Accidentally paid someone's school fees in Croatia.

---

107. I put ".com" at the end of everything now.
Dinner.com
Laundry.com
Silenceplease.com

---

108. Your grandma used the voice assistant.
Now it only speaks Spanish.

---

109. Wi-Fi password: "Don'tAskMe123"

---

110. They said to clear my cache.
I emptied the cookie jar instead.

Dad vs the Internet

111. YouTube asked, "Are you still watching?"
Of course not. I've been asleep since 2011.

---

112. Asked Alexa to play some classics.
She played dial-up internet sounds.

---

113. Siri called me "Bro."
I'm both flattered and offended.

---

114. I joined a Zoom call early.
Had a full-on conversation with myself.

---

115. Instagram asked me to create a reel.
So I fixed the lawnmower.

---

116. Tried online banking.
Now the bank is trying me.

---

117. I sent your mom a GIF.
She thought it was a virus and unplugged the fridge.

---

118. Tried to unsubscribe from emails.
Subscribed to three more instead.

---

119. Facebook said "Happy Friendiversary."
I haven't seen that guy since 1996.

---

120. Your mom tagged me in a post.
Now everyone thinks I sell herbal tea.

Dad vs the Internet

121. Tried Google Docs.
Typed "Dear Diary" and spilled my secrets to HR.

---

122. I downloaded an app to help me sleep.
It screamed at me to stop eating at 2 AM.

---

123. The internet said to "clear my history."
So I burned my yearbook.

---

124. I keep refreshing the Wi-Fi like it owes me rent.

---

125. Your mom thinks cookies are for eating.
Now she's banned from my browser.

---

126. Posted a selfie with the caption "#WokeUpLikeThis."
Lost 12 followers and my job.

---

127. I tried to send a GIF.
Accidentally proposed to someone in Brazil.

---

128. Set up my smart TV.
Now it's watching me.

---

129. Facebook marketplace is wild.
Just traded our blender for a goat.

---

130. Asked ChatGPT for advice.
Now I'm arguing with a robot.

Dad vs the Internet

131. Your cousin said I should get on Threads.
I asked if it was sewing-related.

132. Zoom froze mid-meeting.
I kept nodding like a bobblehead for 20 minutes.

133. AutoCorrect changed "dad" to "mad."
Coincidence? I think not.

134. I bought crypto.
Now I own half a lizard in the metaverse.

135. Said "Hey Google, turn on the lights."
It ordered 10 LED bulbs to the house.

136. Instagram keeps suggesting skincare products.
What are they trying to say??

137. My password is so secure…
Even I don't know it.

138. Tried a "two-step verification."
Tripped on the first step.

139. Clicked "Accept All Cookies."
Still no cookies.
Scam.

140. Asked for tech support.
Got a 13-year-old named Kevin.

Dad's Joke Hall of Shame

The absolute worst ones.

The groaners.

The unholy puns.

Proceed with caution.

WARNING: The following jokes are so bad, they've been officially banned in 6 countries.

Dad's Joke Hall of Shame

1. Parallel lines have so much in common...

(This one was caught trying to sneak into a geometry class.)

2. I used to hate facial hair...
but then it grew on me.

Judge's Gavel Slam: "You are sentenced to 5 years of awkward beard puns."

3. I asked the librarian if the library had books on paranoia...
She whispered, "They're right behind you."

This joke is being watched. Very closely.

4. I told my wife she was drawing her eyebrows too high.
She looked surprised.

5. I'm reading a book about anti-gravity.
It's impossible to put down.

6. I used to play piano by ear...
But now I use my hands.

7. I ordered a chicken and an egg from Amazon.
I'll let you know.

8. I got hit in the head with a can of soda.
But it was a soft drink.

9. I told my suitcase there would be no vacation this year.
Now I'm dealing with emotional baggage.

Dad's Joke Hall of Shame

10. I accidentally swallowed food coloring.
Now I feel like I've dyed a little inside.

11. I don't trust stairs.
They're always up to something.

12. I have a joke about construction...
But I'm still working on it.

13. I bought shoes from a drug dealer.
I don't know what he laced them with, but I've been tripping all day.

14. I used to be addicted to soap.
But now I'm clean.

15. I asked the gym instructor if he could teach me to do the splits.
He replied, "How flexible are you?" I said, "I can't make it on Tuesdays."

16. I named my dog "Five Miles."
So I can say I walk Five Miles every day.

17. I have a fear of speed bumps...
But I'm slowly getting over it.

18. I lost my job as a banker... Because I lost interest.

19. I used to be a baker... But I couldn't make enough dough.

20. I once dated a girl who was a magnet.
She was very attractive.

Dad's Joke Hall of Shame

21. I'm friends with all electricians.
We have good current connections.

22. I started a band called 999 Megabytes.
We haven't gotten a gig yet.

23. I'd tell you a chemistry joke…
But I know I wouldn't get a reaction.

24. I don't play soccer because I enjoy the sport.
I'm just doing it for kicks.

25. I used to work in a calendar factory.
I got fired for taking a few days off.

26. I told my wife she should embrace her mistakes.
She hugged me.

27. I'm on a seafood diet.
I see food and I eat it.

28. I gave all my dead batteries away today.
Free of charge.

29. I had to sell my vacuum cleaner.
It was just gathering dust.

30. I asked the barber if he could make my hair look like a lion's mane.
He said he was afraid to take on that responsibility.

Dad's Joke Hall of Shame

31. I bought a ceiling fan the other day.
Complete waste of money. He just stands there and claps.

32. I once tried to start a hot air balloon business...
But it never really took off.

33. I can't believe I got fired from the calendar factory.
All I did was take a day off... again.

34. My wife asked me to stop impersonating a flamingo.
I had to put my foot down.

35. I told my plants I wouldn't water them anymore.
Now I'm dealing with some serious root issues.

36. I'm so good at sleeping...
I can do it with my eyes closed.

37. I've got a pen that writes underwater.
It can also write other words too.

38. I tried writing with a broken pencil.
Pointless.

39. I couldn't figure out why the baseball kept getting bigger...
Then it hit me.

40. I used to be a tailor...
But I just wasn't suited for it.

Dad's Joke Hall of Shame

41. I wanted to be a doctor, but I didn't have the patients.

42. I got caught stealing a calendar once…
I got twelve months.

43. I told my dad to embrace his mistakes.
He cried and hugged me.

44. I once met a guy who was a claustrophobic astronaut.
He needed a little space.

45. I tried to organize a hide and seek contest…
But it was hard to find good players.

46. I ate a clock yesterday.
It was very time-consuming.

47. The shovel was a ground-breaking invention.

48. The rotation of the earth really makes my day.

49. I made a pencil with two erasers.
It was pointless.

50. I changed my iPod's name to Titanic.
It's syncing now.

Your Official Dad Joke License

Thanks for Surviving This Book

Wow. You made it.
You laughed (maybe). You groaned (definitely). You probably questioned your life choices.

You now have full dad joke immunity.
Use your powers responsibly… or don't.

Now it's your turn:
Write your own worst dad joke below:

"_____"

WARNING: We're not responsible for any emotional damage caused by your joke.

www.ingramcontent.com/pod-product-compliance
Lightning Source LLC
Chambersburg PA
CBHW060357050426
42449CB00009B/1774